Presented to

_____

By

_____

Date

_____

The holy moly STORY BIBLE

EXPLORING GOD'S AWESOME WORD

BY REBECCA GLASER

ILLUSTRATED BY BILL FERENC AND EMMA TRITHART

SPARK HOUSE FAMILY

MINNEAPOLIS

24 23 22 21 20 19 18 17 16 15   1 2 3 4 5 6 7 8

ISBN: 978-1-4514-9988-9

Book design by Toolbox Studios, Dave Wheeler, Alisha Lofgren, and Janelle Markgren
Cover design by Alisha Lofgren
Edited by Erin Gibbons

Library of Congress Cataloging-in-Publication Data

Glaser, Rebecca Stromstad.
 The holy moly story Bible : exploring God's awesome word / by Rebecca Glaser ; illustrated by Bill Ferenc and Emma Trithart.
     pages cm
  ISBN 978-1-4514-9988-9 (alk. paper)
 1. Bible stories, English. I. Ferenc, Bill, illustrator. II. Trithart, Emma, illustrator. III. Title.
  BS551.3.G56 2015
  220.95'05—dc23
                              2015013392

Printed on acid-free paper
Printed in U.S.A.
V63474; 9781451499889; AUG2015

Welcome to

When asked, "What do you think Moses looked like?" how might you respond? Would your response reflect how a child in your life might draw or describe Moses?

In *The Holy Moly Story Bible*, people and places from the Bible are brought to life in creative new ways through images and words. Created in partnership with the hilarious Holy Moly videos, kid-style drawings use elements of humor and unique features and shapes to engage kids as they look, listen, and read these beloved Bible stories. Each story invites readers to enjoy a creative retelling of it, plus respond to the story with a coloring or drawing activity.

Experience something new each time you read a story with a child, either through the words and the captivating illustrations or in the coloring and drawing activities. Grow together in faith as you explore God's awesome Word together.

Holy Moly!

Stories from the Old Testament

Stories from the New Testament

Creation

In the beginning, there was nothing, until God created the heavens and the earth. "Let there be light!" God commanded. And light sparkled across the water. God named light day and darkness night.

At the end of Day 1, God admired creation and said, "It is good."

On Day 2, God placed a bright blue sky high above the water.

Color in the sky.

Splish, splash! Dry land popped up from the water on Day 3. Green plants, tall trees, and colorful flowers burst from the earth.

God made the big, bright sun to shine during the day and the round, pale moon to shine at night. Stars twinkled all across the night sky on Day 4.

On Day 5, the water in the seas bubbled and gurgled and filled with fish. High in the sky, birds chirped and squawked and soared through the air.

Creeping and crawling, hopping and running, animals of every kind filled the earth on Day 6. Lions roared. Cats meowed. Horses neighed.

"Now," said God, "I will make people in my image."
God created a man and a woman. God blessed
them and put them in charge of caring for all of creation.

After six days of hustle and toil,
God took one day to rest.
God blessed Day 7 and made it holy.

With a smile and a laugh,
God looked over all of creation
and said, "It is very good!"

Adam and Eve

The first people God created were named Adam and Eve. They lived in the garden of Eden, where they had everything they needed. God had just one rule:

"You may eat fruit from any tree, except this one in the middle of the garden."

One grim day a serpent slithered up to Eve.

"Thisss tree has the sssweetest fruitsss!" the serpent hissed. *"Try sssome."*

"But God says no!" Eve replied. "If we eat that fruit, we will die!"

"You won't die," the serpent said. *"Eat the fruit from this tree in the middle of the garden. Then you'll know what'sss good and what'sss evil. You'll be like God!"*

Count the fruit on the tree.

Eve picked a fruit from the tree. **CRUNCH!** She took a juicy bite, then passed the fruit to Adam. **CHOMP!** Adam chewed and swallowed.

Gasp! Adam and Eve realized they were naked! They covered their bodies with leaves and hid.

"Where are you?" God called. Adam jumped up and blamed Eve. Eve leapt out and blamed the serpent. They hung their heads in shame.

God punished the serpent and Adam and Eve for breaking the one rule. After creating clothes for Adam and Eve, God sent them out of the perfect garden into the world. God would be with them there too.

Noah

God's creation grew and grew. But the people forgot about God. They fought with each other and destroyed things. They worshipped beings other than God.

In the entire world, only one man remembered God. His name was Noah. God said to Noah:

"I am going to flood the whole earth. Everything will be washed away. Build a giant boat—an ark! Fill it with two of every living animal."

"Do everything I have told you, and I will save you and your family."

Noah obeyed God. He sawed wood and hammered nails. Board by board, Noah built the ark.

Two at a time, animals waddled, stomped, and crawled onto the ark. When all the animals were aboard the ark, Noah and his family went inside.

Kerplunk, drip, splash! The rain began to fall.

Draw other animals that might have been on the ark.

It rained, and poured, and rained some more. The water rose higher and higher. The ark rocked back and forth. Everyone inside stayed dry.

After forty days, the rain stopped. Noah sent a dove to search for dry land.

When all the earth was dry,
God placed a rainbow in the sky.

"I will never flood the whole earth again,"
God promised. "This rainbow is a reminder
of my promise!"

Abraham

Abraham and his wife, Sarah, were faithful to God, but they were worried. Even though God had promised them a baby, they didn't have one. They were old—old enough to be grandparents or even great-grandparents. When would God's promise come true?

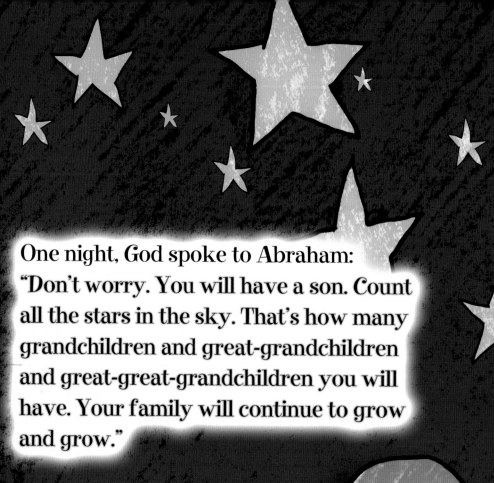

One night, God spoke to Abraham: "Don't worry. You will have a son. Count all the stars in the sky. That's how many grandchildren and great-grandchildren and great-great-grandchildren you will have. Your family will continue to grow and grow."

How many stars do you count? 38

Abraham and Sarah would have to wait many more years for their baby, but they trusted in God's promise.

Sarah and Abraham

One blazing hot afternoon, God sent three men to visit Abraham. When Abraham spotted them, he jumped up. "Hurry!" he called to Sarah. "Make bread for our guests!" Abraham rushed to prepare some meat.

Fill the sky with pictures of food you like to share with guests.

Abraham served the visitors, then sat down with them. **Splash!** The visitors washed their feet. **Slurp!** They drank the milk. **Chomp!** They ate the fresh meat.

"Where is your wife, Sarah?" the men asked. "Soon she will have a son!"

But God keeps promises.
Soon Sarah was expecting
a child. When the baby was
born, Abraham and Sarah
named him Isaac.

Rebekah and Isaac

When Abraham and Sarah's son, Isaac, grew up, Abraham knew it was time for Isaac to get married.

Abraham went to his chief servant. "Go to my homeland," Abraham said. "Find a wife for my son Isaac."

The servant took the camels and traveled a long way to find Abraham's people.

After a long journey to Abraham's homeland, the servant stopped by a well and prayed. "God, help me find a wife for Isaac. If a woman offers a drink of water to me AND to my camels, let her be the one."

Just then, a woman named Rebekah came to the well. She offered water to Abraham's servant AND to his camels! The servant knew Rebekah would become Isaac's wife.

The servant asked Rebekah and her family if she would marry Isaac. They said YES! Rebekah traveled back with Abraham's servant.

Soon Isaac and Rebekah got married, and God blessed them.

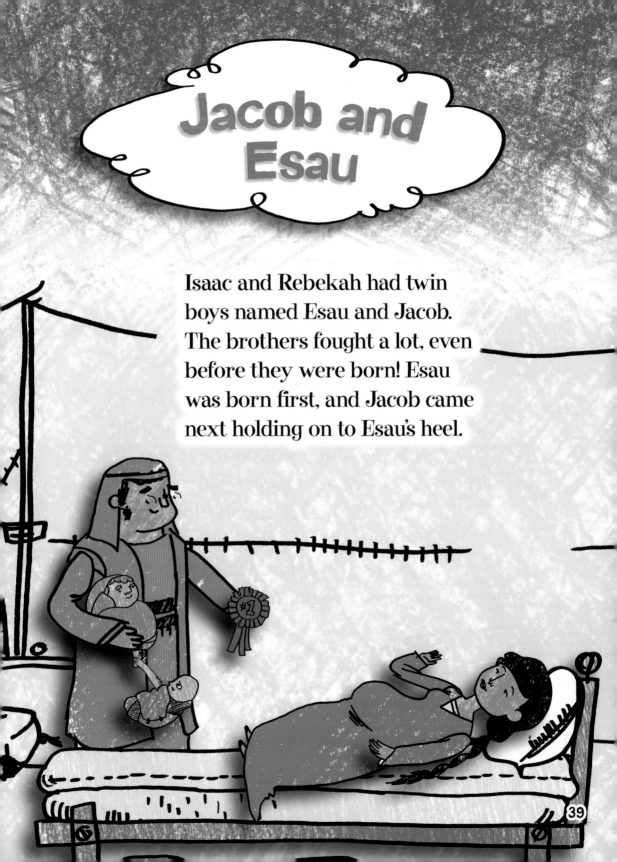

Jacob and Esau

Isaac and Rebekah had twin boys named Esau and Jacob. The brothers fought a lot, even before they were born! Esau was born first, and Jacob came next holding on to Esau's heel.

The brothers were very different. Hairy Esau loved to hunt. Smooth-skinned Jacob liked to stay by the tents. Esau was Isaac's favorite, but Rebekah loved Jacob most. Because Esau was the oldest, he would someday receive his father's blessing for the firstborn.

One day, Esau was very hungry.
He asked Jacob for stew.
"First let me have your blessing,"
Jacob said.

"Okay, you can be number one,"
Esau said. "Just let me eat!"

When Isaac was very old and couldn't see, he told Esau it was time to give his blessing. Rebekah overheard and rushed to Jacob. "Psst," Rebekah whispered. "It's time to take your father's blessing."

While Esau was hunting, Jacob put on Esau's clothes. He covered his arms in hairy goatskin and went to his father.

"Who's there?" Isaac asked.
"It's Esau," Jacob lied.
Isaac felt Jacob's hairy arms and smelled him. The disguise worked! Isaac gave Jacob his blessing. Now Jacob was number one!

Color in Jacob as he's being blessed.

Esau was furious with Jacob! Afraid, Jacob ran far away from home.

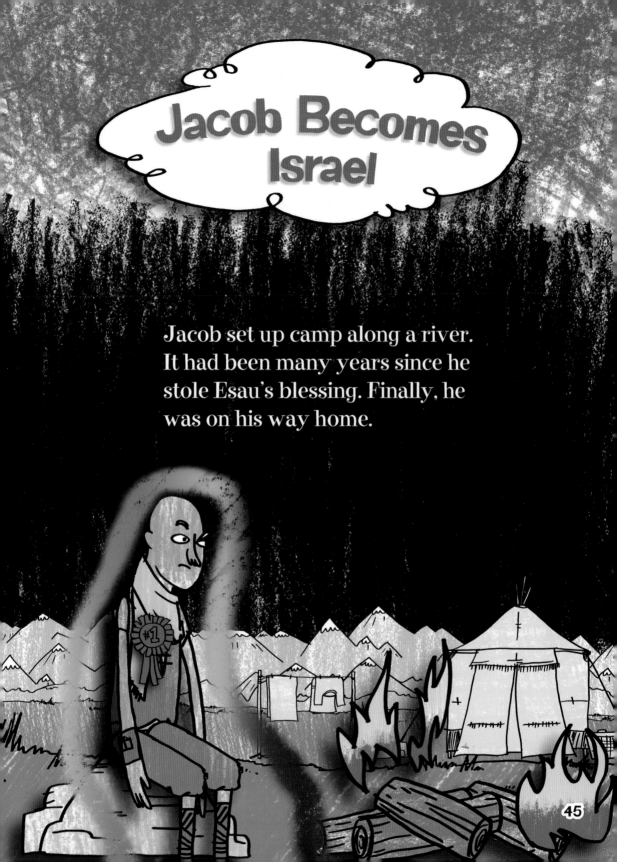

Jacob Becomes Israel

Jacob set up camp along a river. It had been many years since he stole Esau's blessing. Finally, he was on his way home.

It was dark and quiet, and Jacob was alone.
Suddenly a man appeared and grabbed him.
Left, right, up, down! Punch, kick, grapple, fight!
Jacob wrestled the mysterious man ALL night.

Just when the sun was peeking over the horizon, the man knocked Jacob's hip out of its socket.
"Let me go!" the man demanded.
"First, give me a blessing," Jacob said.
"What's your name?" the man asked.
"Jacob," he replied.
"I will give you a new name," the man said. "You will be called Israel because you have struggled with God and won."
Then God blessed Jacob.

The next day, Jacob limped away amazed. "Wow!" he thought. "I met God face-to-face!"

Draw a bandage on Jacob's hip.

Joseph and His Brothers

1, 2, 3, 4, 5, 6, 7, 8, 9, 10, 11, 12!
Jacob had twelve sons. But he
had one favorite—Joseph.
Jacob gave Joseph a big, beautiful robe.
The eleven other brothers
were jealous!

One night Joseph dreamed that stars and grain bowed to him. He realized that someday, his family would bow down to him the same way the stars and grain did. Joseph's dream made his brothers angry!

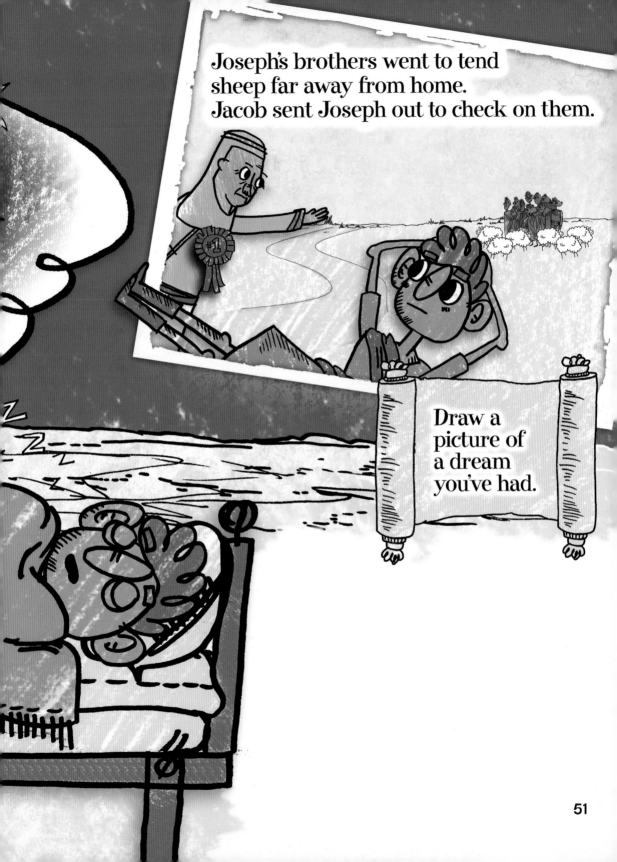

Joseph's brothers went to tend sheep far away from home. Jacob sent Joseph out to check on them.

Draw a picture of a dream you've had.

Joseph's angry brothers plotted to get rid of him. When they saw him coming, they grabbed Joseph and tore off his fancy robe.

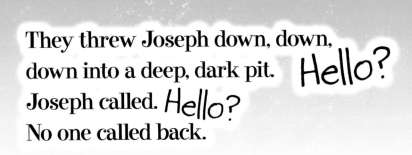

They threw Joseph down, down,
down into a deep, dark pit. Hello?
Joseph called. Hello?
No one called back.

Just then, a trader passed by. Not wanting to kill Joseph, the brothers decided to sell him to the trader. "Then we'll be rid of him for good," they said.

The trader took Joseph to Egypt, where he sold Joseph to work for one of Pharaoh's officers.

Joseph Interprets Pharaoh's Dream

Pharaoh, the ruler of Egypt, was worried about his dreams. In one dream, seven thin cows ate seven plump ones. In another, seven dying stalks of grain swallowed up seven healthy ones. Pharaoh wondered . . .

"WHAT do these dreams MEAN?"

Pharaoh called
all his wise men and
magicians together. "Please,
tell me what my dreams mean!"
Pharaoh pleaded.
But nobody knew.

Color in
Pharaoh's
dream.

56

Then one of Pharaoh's servants had an idea. "I know a man who can tell you what your dreams mean!" he said.

The servant rushed to get Joseph and bring him to Pharaoh. Joseph was worried! What did Pharaoh want?
"Tell me what my dreams mean!" Pharaoh demanded.

Relieved, Joseph nodded and said, "The meaning of your dreams won't come from me but from God. Egypt will have seven years of food galore. But then, there will be seven years of no food at all. Store up food during the years of plenty, and eat it during the years of famine."

59

Pharaoh was astounded! He made Joseph a great ruler in Egypt and put him in charge of storing food. For seven years, they collected food to store. So when there was no more food to gather, they still had enough to eat!

Joseph Forgives

Famine spread far and wide across the land outside Egypt. Crops couldn't grow. There wasn't anything to eat. People traveled from all over to buy food from Egypt.

Far away, Joseph's family was running out of food. Jacob sent his sons to buy grain in Egypt. They didn't know their brother Joseph was a great ruler there who controlled all the food supplies!

When the brothers came to ask for food,
Joseph recognized them right away.
The brothers bowed down to Joseph,
just like in his dreams from long ago.

Joseph jumped up and exclaimed,
"It's me, your lost brother!
Is our father still alive?
Bring him here too!"

Joseph's brothers were amazed and shocked! They raced to bring Jacob to Egypt. Jacob couldn't wait to see his favorite son again!

Joseph rushed to give his father a big hug. "I missed you so much!" he cried. Filled with joy, Jacob embraced his son. Father, son, and the eleven brothers were finally reunited.

Baby Moses

Pharaoh was angry, and Pharaoh was mean. He made a law to get rid of all the Israelite baby boys. One mother was determined to save her son.

She made a papyrus basket and nestled her baby boy inside.

Gently, the mother placed the basket in the river. Miriam, the baby's older sister, watched as the basket floated away.

The basket bobbed up and down along the river to where Pharaoh's daughter was bathing in the water. She peeked inside the basket. "This must be a Israelite baby!" she exclaimed. "I'll raise him as my son!"

Draw a baby in the basket.

Miriam knew just what to do. She jumped up and said, "I know someone who can help care for your baby!" She rushed to get her mother.

Pharaoh's daughter gave the baby to Miriam and her mother to bring home. The baby's family smiled BIG smiles. He was safe!

When the boy grew older, he went to live with Pharaoh's daughter. She named him Moses because she "drew him out of water."

Crossing the Red Sea

When Moses grew up, the Israelites, God's chosen people, were still slaves in Egypt. Pharaoh forced them to work very hard. But God had chosen Moses to free the Israelites from slavery.

God sent Moses to Pharaoh. "The Lord says, 'Let my people go!'" Moses told Pharaoh. But Pharaoh refused. Ten times Moses asked, and each time, Pharaoh said, "No!" After each no, God sent a plague to Egypt.

1. The river waters turned to blood.
2. Frogs hopped over all the land.
3. Clouds of gnats filled the air.
4. Swarms of flies flew inside and out.
5. The animals got sick and died.
6. Sores covered the Egyptians' skin.
7. Thunder boomed, and hail rained down.
8. Locusts ate the plants and trees.
9. Darkness came for three days and nights.
10. Firstborn Egyptian children died.

Finally, Pharaoh let the Israelites go!
Moses led the people away, but at the edge
of the Red Sea, they heard Pharaoh's army
approaching. They were trapped!

Color in
the sea.

Moses called out over the crowd:
"Do not be afraid. God is with us!"
He raised his staff, and God divided
the waters. The Israelites hurried
across the Red Sea on dry land.

When the Israelites were safe on the other side, the sea crashed back down. Pharaoh's army was swept away. The Israelites cheered with joy. "We're safe! God has rescued us!"

The Ten Commandments

Moses climbed up, up, up Mount Sinai.
At the tip-top, God spoke to him.
Moses listened to God's important
message for the Israelites.

"Respect your father and mother."

"Do not harm anyone."

"Husbands and wives, be faithful to each other."

"Do not take things that aren't yours."

"Do not tell lies."

"Do not be jealous of your neighbor's things."

Write down a rule that you follow:

eat I

Moses brought God's ten important rules to the people on two stone tablets. God's commandments helped the Israelites learn how to live with each other and with God.

Brave Deborah

Deborah had an important job. God chose her to be a judge to help lead the Israelites. When the Israelites had a disagreement or problem, they would go find Deborah under her palm tree and ask for help.

A general named Sisera was hurting the Israelites. God told Deborah it was time to defeat Sisera's army.

Deborah called a soldier named Barak. "God wants you to lead an army to defeat Sisera," she told him.

How does God help you? Draw a picture of one way.

Stay together

Barak shook with fear. "If YOU go with me, I will go," he told Deborah.

Deborah trusted God and agreed to go. She and Barak led an army to fight Sisera. With God's help, they defeated Sisera's army!

Naomi and Ruth

Naomi lived in the country of Moab with her two sons and their wives, Orpah and Ruth.

One sad day, Naomi's sons died. Naomi, Ruth, and Orpah didn't know what to do! They didn't have any food or money of their own.

The three women decided to make the long journey back to Naomi's home country of Judah.

But Naomi realized Judah would be a strange, faraway land to Orpah and Ruth. "Go back to your families," she told them. "May God bless you with new husbands." Orpah kissed Naomi and went back to her family.

But Ruth grabbed Naomi's hand. "I won't leave you!" she said to Naomi. No matter what Naomi said, Ruth wouldn't leave.

Smiling, Ruth assured Naomi,
"Where you go, I'll go.
Where you stay, I'll stay.
Your people will be my people,
and your God will be my God."

Together, Ruth and Naomi
traveled to Judah.

Queen Esther

King Ahasuerus needed a new queen. Of ALL the girls in the land, the king chose Esther to be queen. Queen Esther had a secret—she was Jewish. The king was not.

Mordecai was Esther's cousin. He was Jewish too. He worshipped ONLY God. When Haman, the king's official, demanded that everyone bow down to him, Mordecai refused.

Haman was so angry with Mordecai that he convinced the king to kill ALL the Jewish people. But Mordecai learned of Haman's plan, and he secretly asked Esther to help.

Esther was scared, but she was determined to save her people. Esther bowed down before the king. "Please, you must stop Haman!" she pleaded. "His plan will destroy my people."

The king listened to Queen Esther. The Jewish people were saved! They celebrated a new holiday, called Purim, to remember the day that Esther saved them.

94

God Calls Samuel

Samuel was a boy who lived in the temple with an old priest named Eli. He served Eli, helping him with whatever he needed. One night, when Samuel was sleeping, he heard a voice calling.

(Saaamuuuelll!)

Samuel woke up and rubbed his eyes. He ran to Eli. "Here I am. What do you need?" Samuel asked.
"I didn't call. Go back to sleep," Eli replied.

(Saaamuuuellll!) the voice called again.
Samuel ran to Eli. "Here I am. You called me."
"I didn't call. Go back to sleep," Eli said again.

(Saaamuuuelll!) the voice called a third time. Samuel ran to Eli. This time, Eli realized it was God calling. He told Samuel, "Next time say, 'Speak, Lord. Your servant is listening.'"

Samuel Anoints David

God spoke to the prophet Samuel: "It's time to choose a new king! Fill your horn with oil and go to the family of Jesse. I'll show you who will become the next king of Israel."

Samuel set off to meet Jesse's family and find the new king. When he arrived, he was amazed by Jesse's sons.

Some were big and strong. Others were skilled and smart. Samuel was sure one of these would be the new king.

Thump, thump, thump, thump. Jesse's oldest, biggest son stepped forward. Surely he would make a good king!

After seeing seven sons, Samuel scratched his head. "Are ALL your sons here?" he asked Jesse. "My youngest son, David, is tending the sheep," Jesse replied.

The other sons laughed. "Ha! David's not fit to be king!" "He's too young!" "He's too small!" "He's too stinky!" But Samuel sent them to fetch David.

Draw what you think a king looks like.

When young David stepped forward, God spoke to Samuel: "This is the one. David will be the next king of Israel." Samuel anointed David. He took some oil from his horn and put it on David's head. From that day, God's Spirit stayed with David.

Color in David to show that he received the Spirit of God.

David and Goliath

While David was caring for his sheep, the Israelites were battling the Philistines. In front of the Philistine army stood a mighty BIG man named Goliath. **"Who will fight me?"** Goliath shouted.

Goliath was HUGE! His legs were as big as trees! The Israelites were afraid. No soldier dared fight the giant—not even King Saul.

"I'll do it," David said. The soldiers and King Saul couldn't believe it. How could little David fight **HUGE** Goliath?

King Saul gave David heavy metal armor to wear and a big, sharp sword to fight with. But David realized, "I'm not going to win this fight with a sword! God will protect me!"

David shook off the heavy armor and picked up his sling and five smooth stones.

Goliath laughed. **"Do you think you can defeat me with five little stones?"** he roared.

"I can with God's help," David called back. He ran toward Goliath, loaded his sling, and launched the stone at his enemy.

THWAP!

The stone hit Goliath right in the forehead. **THUD!**

Goliath fell to the ground. David had defeated Goliath! The Philistine army ran away.

HOORAY!

With God's help, young David was a hero!

Daniel and the Lions

Of all the advisors who worked for King Darius, Daniel was the king's favorite. Daniel was an excellent advisor. He was honest, and the king trusted him.

The king's other advisors were jealous. They wanted Daniel to get in trouble, but Daniel never broke any laws. The advisors decided to trick the king into making a new law.

Draw yourself praying to God.

The new law said that EVERYONE had to worship the king. If ANYONE prayed to someone else, they would be thrown into the lions' den.

Daniel worshipped and prayed to ONLY God. The king's advisors knew that Daniel would break the new law.

One day, the advisors caught Daniel praying to God. "GOTCHA!" they shouted. They grabbed him and took him to the lions' den. Even the king couldn't save Daniel!

Daniel tumbled into the pit. A large stone covered the hole so Daniel couldn't escape. He closed his eyes and prayed.

"I worship God, and only God, not kings, not queens—no others on earth," Daniel prayed.

King Darius worried about Daniel all night. In the morning, he hurried to the lions' den. "Has your God rescued you?" the king called down to Daniel.

"I'm safe!" Daniel shouted up to the king. "God sent an angel, who shut the lions' mouths."

Daniel climbed out of the pit. "The lions didn't hurt me because God protected me," he said. "I worship God, and only God, not kings, not queens—no others on earth."

King Darius jumped for joy! He made a new law telling everyone to worship Daniel's God.

Color King Darius.

Jonah and the Big Fish

Jonah was God's prophet. God told him,

"Go to Nineveh! I need you to deliver a message to the people there."

Jonah did NOT want to go. "Who, me? No way! I won't go there!" he said.

Without another word, Jonah ran away. He climbed on a ship and sailed far from Nineveh. God sent a BIG storm that battered the ship.

The worried sailors threw off some cargo and tried to row back to shore. Nothing worked.

Color the fish God sent to swallow Jonah.

The crew pushed Jonah off the ship. SPLASH! Jonah landed in the sea. Right away the storm stopped.

GULP! God sent a large fish to swallow Jonah.

For three days, Jonah waited inside the stinky belly of the fish. He prayed, "God, please get me out of here! I promise to go to Nineveh!"

God heard Jonah's prayer and made the fish spit him out on the beach. "Thank you, God!" Jonah cheered.

Again, God told Jonah, **"Go to Nineveh!"** Jonah faced his fear and followed God's command. He brought God's message to Nineveh.

The Angel Speaks to Mary

Mary lived in the town of Nazareth.
She was engaged to a man named Joseph.

Whoosh Whoosh.

One day, an angel appeared to Mary.

"Greetings!" the angel Gabriel said.

Mary's heart pounded. She gasped with fear. Who was this? And why was he talking to HER?

"Do not be afraid, Mary, for you have found favor with God," Gabriel said. "You will have a son. His name will be Jesus."

Mary was surprised! But she trusted God.

God sent an angel to Joseph in a dream. "Do not be afraid, Joseph," the angel told him. "Take Mary as your wife. She will have a son, and you will name him Jesus."

Mary and Joseph were nervous, but they knew God was with them. They prepared for the birth of God's Son.

Mary and Elizabeth

While Mary was pregnant, she set out to visit her relative Elizabeth. Even though Elizabeth was very old, God had promised she would have a baby too!

Mary walked and walked along the road, through towns and past houses, until she arrived at Elizabeth's house in a town in the hill country of Judea.

Color the path Mary took.

When Elizabeth saw Mary, the baby inside her jumped for joy. "Mary, you are blessed!" Elizabeth exclaimed. "You're going to have God's Son!"

Mary praised God, saying, "My soul celebrates God's greatness! I am blessed as God's servant. God has done wonderful things in my life. Praise God's holy name!"

Mary stayed with Elizabeth for about three months. Elizabeth gave birth to a son and named him John. When John grew up, many people called him John the Baptist.

Jesus Is Born

On the night Jesus was born, there were shepherds nearby. They watched over their flocks of sheep in the fields outside Bethlehem.

135

Mary and Joseph were in Bethlehem for the census, just like many, many other people. All the inns were full, so Mary and Joseph stayed in a stable with animals nearby.

Baby Jesus was born that night. Mary wrapped him in cloth and laid him in a manger.

WHOOSH! An angel appeared before the shepherds in the field. They were frightened and tried to hide!

"Do not be afraid," the angel said. "I bring you good news of great joy. The Messiah, God's Son, was born today!"

Just then the sky was FILLED with angels singing, "Glory to God and peace on Earth!"

The shepherds hurried
off to find the new baby—
the Messiah!

141

At the humble stable, the shepherds found the baby Jesus, Mary, and Joseph. They peeked at the baby's tiny hands. They smiled at the baby's little toes. They were amazed. Jesus, God's Son, had been born!

The Wise Men Follow the Star

A long way from Bethlehem, some wise men were watching the stars. Suddenly, they saw something surprising. A new star was rising! It was a sign that a special king had been born for God's people.

143

The wise men traveled to Jerusalem in search of the new king. They wanted to visit the child and honor him.

King Herod was jealous when he heard. A new king? Herod wanted to be the ONLY king! He searched high and low to find out where this new king was.

Herod called the wise men.
"Go to Bethlehem and find
this new king," he told them.

The wise men followed
the star to Bethlehem.
It shone high in the sky
over a little house where
Jesus, Mary, and Joseph
were staying.

Color in
the map.

When the wise men saw Jesus, they welcomed and honored him with gifts of gold, frankincense, and myrrh. In a dream, they were warned not to tell Herod where the child was, so they went home by a different route.

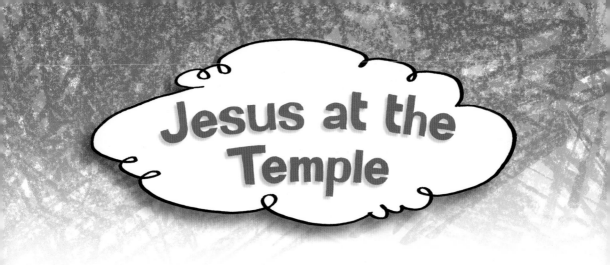

Jesus at the Temple

When Jesus was twelve years old,
he traveled with his family to Jerusalem
to celebrate the Passover festival.
They visited the temple and heard
the story of God rescuing
their ancestors from Egypt.

When the celebration was over, Jesus' family traveled toward home. After one day's journey, Mary and Joseph realized Jesus was missing.

"Joseph, where's Jesus?" Mary exclaimed. "I thought he was with you!" Joseph replied. Mary and Joseph looked high and low for Jesus, but he wasn't with their group. "We've got to go back and find him!" Mary said.

Color in
the stars.

153

Scared and worried,
Mary and Joseph
hurried back to Jerusalem.
They searched for Jesus
for three days. Finally,
they found him in the
temple.

Jesus was talking with the temple teachers. The teachers asked Jesus questions and were amazed by his wisdom.

Mary marched over to Jesus. "We've been searching for you everywhere!" she said angrily.

Jesus answered calmly, "Why were you searching for me? Didn't you know I would be in my Father's house?" Mary and Joseph didn't understand, but they were relieved to have found their son.

John the Baptist

God sent a messenger to get people ready for Jesus. Was it a priest in the temple? No! It was a man called John the Baptist, who lived in the wilderness.

John was a surprising messenger! He wore scratchy camel-hair clothes. He ate crunchy locusts and sweet honey. John told people how to get ready for Jesus. "Confess your sins!" he preached. "Change your ways!"

John waded out into the Jordan River,
and the people followed. One by one,
John baptized each person in the river.
"I baptize you with water," John told them,
"but Jesus will baptize you with the Holy Spirit."

159

One day Jesus came to the Jordan River to be baptized. He waded into the river, and John dunked him into the water. When Jesus came up out of the water, the heavens opened, and the Holy Spirit came down like a dove.

God's voice rang out, "You are my Son, whom I love; with you I am pleased." And still today, baptism assures us of God's love and forgiveness.

Color the people John baptized.

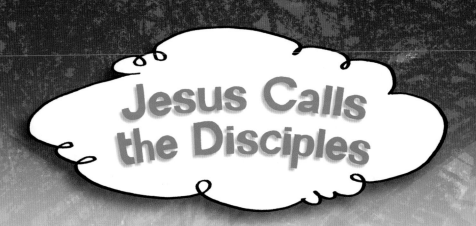

Jesus Calls the Disciples

Jesus traveled to many towns to preach and teach about God. He called followers to help him. Those helpers were called disciples.

One day, Jesus was teaching by the sea. He called out to some men who were fishing in a little boat, "Come, follow me! We'll fish for people instead of fish!"

Simon Peter and Andrew left their boat and followed Jesus.

James and John heard too, and they dropped their fishnet. The first four disciples followed Jesus and wondered what they would learn from him.

Color the disciples named James and John.

163

Jesus called all types of people—even a tax collector named Matthew! "Follow me, and God will make you new," Jesus told him. Matthew left his coins and hurried to follow Jesus.

Along the way, others joined: Philip, Bartholomew, Thomas, Simon, Thaddeus, another man named James, and Judas too. Altogether, Jesus had twelve disciples!

Many others followed Jesus too, and not all of them were men. Mary Magdalene, another woman named Mary, Joanna, Susanna, and many other women said "Yes!" to following Jesus!

Jesus' disciples traveled with him. They learned from Jesus and helped him teach about God.

You can follow Jesus too! Add your own name here.

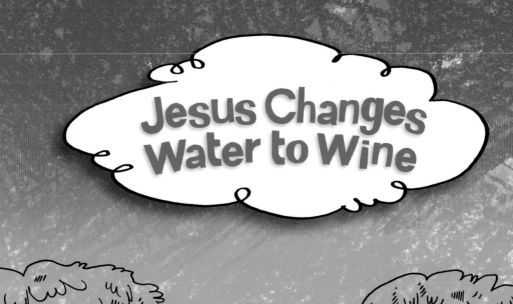

Jesus Changes Water to Wine

Jesus, the disciples, and Jesus' mother, Mary, were all invited to a wedding party! Friends and family came together to celebrate the new husband and wife.

The food was tasty. The wine was sweet. The party was fun! Until . . .

"Oh, no! We're out of wine! What will we do?" cried the wedding host.

Wine is made from grapes. Draw some grapes here.

Mary asked Jesus, "Won't you help them?"
"Not yet!" Jesus replied. "It's not the right time."
But Mary knew he could.

Mary whispered to the servants, "Do whatever Jesus asks you to do."

Jesus saw six large jars. "Fill those jars with water," Jesus said. The servants filled each jar to the brim.

"Now draw some out, and have the host taste it," Jesus told them. The servants brought some to the host.

The host sipped from the goblet, but it wasn't water. Jesus had turned the water into wine—the best wine they'd had all day!

This was Jesus' first of many miracles.

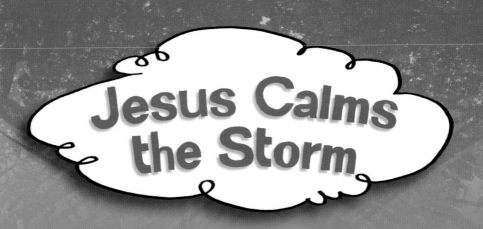

Jesus Calms the Storm

Jesus and his disciples climbed into a boat. With a cool breeze and a small splash, they began to sail smoothly across the sea.

Suddenly, the wind began to blow stronger. The boat was pushed back and forth on the water.

Dark clouds rolled in. Waves splashed over the sides of the boat. The disciples were drenched!

Frightened, the disciples cried out, "Jesus, please save us from the storm!" But Jesus was sound asleep.

Draw Zs to show Jesus sleeping.

Jesus looked calmly at the disciples. "Why are you so scared? Don't you have faith?" he asked.

Standing up, Jesus commanded the wind and waves to stop. Everything became calm and quiet.

The disciples were amazed! They whispered to each other, "Who is this man, that even the wind and the sea obey him?"

The Parable of the House on the Rock

Jesus loved to teach people about God by telling parables. Parables are stories about everyday things, like planting or building, and everyday people, like parents and kids!

One day, Jesus told a parable about two builders to teach about faith.

179

Two men each set out to build a home. The first man climbed up a tall rock. Stomp, stomp! He pounded his foot on the big, strong rock. "I'll build right here on this sturdy foundation!" he said.

Thump thump! Clink clank!

He got to work building his house.

Draw where you would build your home.

The second man wriggled his toes in the soft sand. He didn't want to climb up a big rock. "I'll build my house here on this warm sand," he said. He quickly built his house, then rested in the sun.

Clouds filled the sky, and with a *trickle* and a **drip**, it started to rain. A great **smack** of thunder cracked across the sky. The first man hurried into his house, where it was safe from the storm.

The second man scurried inside too, but the rain and wind knocked his house down!

Just like the man on the rock, God's people should build their faith on a sturdy foundation— God's Word. When we hear and listen to God, our faith becomes strong!

The Parable of the Sower

Jesus told a parable about planting, or sowing, seeds to teach people about listening to God.

A sower's job must be easy, right? Just plant the seeds in the ground. But seeds need lots of things, like sunshine and water and, especially, good soil.

A sower went out to sow one day, scattering and flinging seeds far and wide. Each little seed found its own place to land.

Plink, plunk!

Some of the seeds landed on the smooth path. **Swoosh!** A flock of birds flew down and ate up all those seeds.

The seeds on the path are like a person who hears God but doesn't understand. When we don't understand, we quickly forget!

Some of the seeds landed on rocky ground. **Pop!** They sprouted up quickly but died in the hot sun.

The seeds on rocky ground are like people who listen to God when they're happy but forget God when they're unhappy.

Some of the seeds landed among thorny bushes. **Squish!** The weeds choked the new plants, and they died.

The seeds in the thorns are like people who worry too much and forget to listen to God.

Other seeds fell on good soil. **Grrrrrow!** The plants grew up strong and healthy and made more seeds!

The seeds in good soil are like people who listen to and understand God. They tell everyone about God's word, spreading God's love far and wide.

The Parable of the Mustard Seed

Some of Jesus' followers were curious. "What is the kingdom of God like?" they wondered. Jesus helped them understand by telling a parable about a mustard seed.

A mustard seed is tiny! Color the seeds.

The kingdom of God is like a mustard seed. It starts out tiny. But when it's planted, it grows into a HUGE mustard tree.

The big mustard tree has lots of room on its branches for birds to nest in its shade.

The kingdom of God has room for ALL God's people to live and be safe.

The Parable of the Good Samaritan

People knew they should love their neighbors, but many Jewish people and Samaritans did NOT like each other. So Jesus told a parable to teach about neighbors.

A Jewish man walked along the road to Jericho. Suddenly, a group of robbers attacked him. They hurt him, stole his money, and left him lying by the side of the road.

A priest walked along the road toward the hurt man. The man called out for help, but the priest looked the other direction.

"He's not my neighbor. No time to stop!" the priest thought as he hurried away.

Soon, the man saw a woman and her son coming near. But the woman reacted just like the priest.

"He's not my neighbor. I'd better keep going!" she thought as she rushed away.

Another person was walking toward the man. Oh, no! A Samaritan! The man worried that the Samaritan would hurt him too. But the Samaritan knelt down next to the man and helped him up.

"You're my neighbor. I'll bandage your wounds and find you a safe place to rest," the Samaritan said.

The Samaritan brought the hurt man to an inn and paid the innkeeper to care for him until he was healed.

Neighbors help people in need—not just their family and friends. The Samaritan man helped the Jewish man, even though Samaritans and Jewish people didn't like each other. Jesus taught that we should all be neighbors to each other—even people we don't like!

The Parable of the Prodigal Son

Jesus told a parable about two sons and their father to help people understand God's love.

A father had two sons. The younger son dreamed of going on an adventure. "Father," he asked, "can I have my inheritance early, so I can travel far away?"

The father agreed and gave the younger son his inheritance. A few days later, the son set out on his journey.

In a faraway country, the younger son spent his inheritance on parties and clothes and expensive food.

The older son stayed home and worked hard for his father. He plowed and cleaned and cared for the animals.

After a short time, the younger brother ran out of money. He took a job feeding pigs, but he realized the pigs had better food than he did! He was muddy and miserable.

Draw how you would feel if you were the older brother.

The son missed his home and his family, but he knew he didn't deserve to go back. "Maybe my father will let me be his servant," he thought. He decided to go home.

When his son arrived home, the father was filled with joy. "Welcome home!" he cheered.

The older son was NOT joyful. "Why are you happy to see him?" he complained.

"I thought your brother was lost, but now he is found," the father explained. "Let's celebrate!"

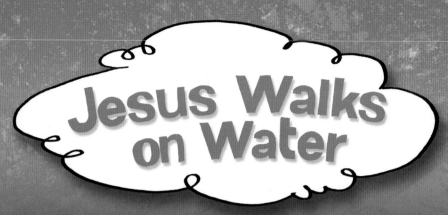

Jesus Walks on Water

Jesus sent the disciples across the sea in a boat so he could pray by himself. As night fell, strong winds blew the boat far away from shore. In the dark, the disciples spotted a shadow coming toward the boat. "It's a ghost!" they yelled in fear.

The shadow got bigger and bigger.
"It's getting closer!" the disciples shouted.
They peered out at the ghostly figure. It
had legs. And arms. And hair! It was a man.
A man walking on the water with no boat
to hold him! "Don't be afraid," the figure
said. "It's me—Jesus!"

Color a path
from Jesus to
the boat.

"Jesus, tell me to walk on the water with you!" said Peter. Jesus waved to Peter. "Come here!" he called. Peter's heart beat like a drum, but he stepped out onto the water.

Step by step, Peter walked toward Jesus,
trusting he wouldn't sink.
The other disciples watched, amazed!
Peter was walking on water!

Just then, a strong gust of wind blew,
and Peter gasped and looked away.
In that short moment,
Peter began to sink!

The water rose past his ankles, then
his knees, then his hips! "Jesus, save me!"
Peter cried. Jesus grabbed Peter's hand
and pulled him out of the water.

Jesus helped Peter back into the boat.
"Where's your faith?" he asked.
"Why did you doubt?"
The disciples were amazed and said,
"Jesus, you really are the Son of God!"

A Man through the Roof

Two men carried a third man on a mat. He was paralyzed and couldn't walk. The two men hoped Jesus could heal their friend, so they walked a long way to meet him.

Color the people who came to see Jesus.

The men spotted Jesus.
He was teaching inside
a house—a house filled
wall-to-wall with people!
The men were worried.
How would they get in?

They pushed on the door,
but it didn't budge.
They peeked through the window,
but there was no room!
They checked for another door,
but there wasn't one!

"We've come this far.
We can't give up now.
We've got to find a way!"
the men said.

"I have an idea!" one yelled. "Let's try the roof!" They boosted their friend up, then climbed up after him. Scratching and pounding, they made a big hole.

Down through the hole they lowered their friend. He landed right in front of Jesus. Amazed at the faith of the friends, Jesus said, "Your sins are forgiven."

"Stand, take your mat, and go home," Jesus told the man. The paralyzed man hopped up from his mat. He could walk again! The friends cheered! All the people were astonished and praised God.

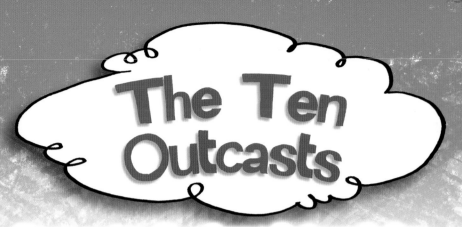

The Ten Outcasts

Jesus was traveling along a dusty road when he saw ten people who were sick with leprosy. Their skin was covered in bright red bumps. Because of their sickness, the ten people weren't allowed to be around anyone who was healthy, not even their families!

The sick people hurried over to Jesus.
"Have mercy!" they called to him.
"Please heal our skin!"

Jesus replied, "Go and show
yourselves to the priests."
Filled with hope, the ten
people hurried off to see
the priests.

One man skidded to a stop.
He looked at his hands.
They were smooth and clean.
He looked at his arms.
No red bumps! "Look!"
he shouted to his friends.
"Our skin is healed! Hooray!"

Color in the other
people who were
healed by Jesus.

Nine of the healed people ran to the priests. But the man who had stopped ran in the opposite direction. He fell down at Jesus' feet. "Thank you! Praise God! We're healed!"

Jesus looked at the man. "Weren't there ten of you? Where are the others?" he asked. Then he told him, "Go now. Your faith has made you well."

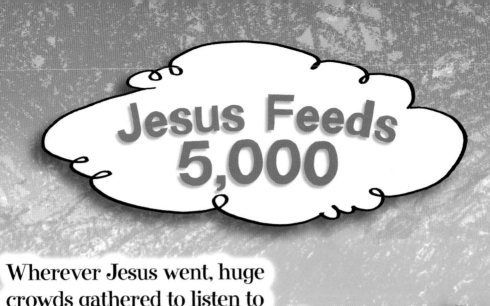

Jesus Feeds 5,000

Wherever Jesus went, huge crowds gathered to listen to him. One day, there was a crowd of 5,000 people. And it was almost time for lunch!

Philip was shocked. "Six months' wages couldn't buy enough bread for everyone!" he replied.

The disciple Andrew spoke up. "This boy has some food."

The disciples looked in the boy's basket. There were only five loaves of bread and two fish. "That's not enough to feed 5,000 people!" they said.

Color and count the loaves and fish.

225

Jesus told the crowd to sit down on the grass. He said a prayer of thanks for the food and began to hand out bread and fish.

The crowd passed the bread and fish from person to person. "Nom, nom, nom," they munched. There was plenty of food! Everyone ate until they were full!

"Gather up what's left," Jesus told the disciples. They were surprised! Enough food for everyone AND leftovers? It was a miracle!

The leftovers filled twelve baskets!
All the people in the crowd were
amazed and whispered to each
other, "Jesus really is the prophet!"

Lazarus

Mary and Martha were sad. Their brother, Lazarus, was sick. They knew he would soon die. They sent a message to Jesus: "Come quickly! Heal your friend Lazarus before he is gone!"

The message reached Jesus, but he didn't come soon enough. Lazarus died. Mary and Martha wrapped his body in strips of cloth and placed him in a tomb.

Lazarus had already been dead for four days. But the two sisters went with Jesus to their brother's tomb.

They rolled the stone away from the opening.

Closing his eyes, Jesus prayed, "Father, thank you for always hearing me. Help this crowd hear, see, and believe!"

With a loud voice, Jesus commanded, "Lazarus, come out!"

The crowd gasped. Still covered in the strips of cloth, Lazarus walked out of the tomb. He was alive again! The sisters rushed to remove the cloth.

Filled with joy, Mary and Martha hugged their brother.

Because of this miracle, many of the people believed in Jesus.

The Lord's Prayer

Jesus wanted to help people learn how to pray. "Talk with God," Jesus said. "God is listening! And you can listen for God too."

"Start by praying these words," Jesus said.

Our Father in heaven, hallowed be your name.

Hallowed means "holy." We honor God's name because God is holy.

Your kingdom come, your will be done, on earth as in heaven.

God's kingdom is where we experience God's love and follow God's ways. God's kingdom is in heaven, but it's here on earth too!

Give us this day our daily bread.
Ask God for what you need today.

Forgive us our sins, as we forgive those who sin against us.
Admit the things you've done wrong. Ask for forgiveness, and forgive others.

Lead us not into temptation, but deliver us from evil.
God is greater than hard times or bad things. God is always with us.

My Prayer

Write or draw a prayer of your own.

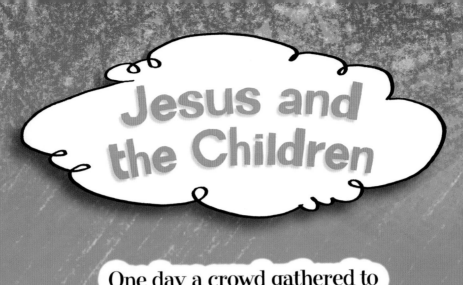

Jesus and the Children

One day a crowd gathered to listen to Jesus. Some parents brought their children to meet Jesus so he would bless them.

The kids played and laughed. They couldn't sit still. They wanted to see Jesus!

"No, no!" said Jesus. "I love kids! Let them come to me. Don't stop them. They are part of God's family too!"

243

The children ran to Jesus and hugged him. Jesus smiled and laughed. He gathered all the children in his arms and blessed them.

The Widow's Offering

Jesus was with his disciples at the temple. They watched and listened as many people gave their temple offerings.

CRASH!
The richest people gave
huge sacks of coins!
They smiled proudly at
their offerings.

A widow came to the temple to give her offering. **Plink! Plink!** She gave two coins, the only coins she had. Quietly, she hurried back outside and went home.

The widow's coins were smaller than pennies. Color the coins.

249

Jesus asked the disciples, "Which offering was the greatest?"

The disciples remembered the huge sacks of coins. "The BIG offerings will help A LOT," the disciples replied.

"The rich people gave BIG offerings, but it was just a LITTLE of all they had," Jesus explained. "The widow gave ALL she had, just two coins. Her offering was the greatest of all."

Mary and Martha

Mary and Martha were excited. Jesus and his disciples were coming to visit! The sisters couldn't wait to welcome Jesus into their home.

Martha spent all day getting ready for the guests. She stirred and cooked the food; she washed and dried the dishes. "There's so much to do!" she exclaimed. "Why isn't Mary helping me?"

Finally, their guests arrived. Mary was so excited! She sat right at Jesus' feet, waiting to hear him teach.

Martha stomped into the room.

"I've done my share of the work today," Martha grumbled. "Let Mary help!"

Color Mary sitting at Jesus' feet.

Jesus turned to Martha and said, "Martha, you are worried about too many things. You only need to do one thing: learn about God! Mary has already chosen to listen, and I won't stop her."

Zacchaeus the Tax Collector

"He's coming! He's coming!" the crowds cheered. People lined the streets of Jericho to see Jesus.

On the tips of his toes, stretched high as he could, Zacchaeus tried to see over the crowd. But he was too short.

Zacchaeus was a tax collector. Sometimes he collected the right amount. Other times he took extra and kept it for himself. The people of Jericho didn't like Zacchaeus and wouldn't help him.

Zacchaeus spotted a sycamore tree with branches reaching high above the crowd. He shimmied up the trunk and sat down on a big branch. But where was Jesus?

"Zacchaeus, hurry down from there! I'm going to your house today!" a voice called. Zacchaeus looked down. It was Jesus! Zacchaeus slid down from the tree.

Zacchaeus waved his arms. "Wait!" he shouted. "I will pay everyone back times four. I will give away half of what I have!"

Jesus smiled at Zacchaeus. "This is why I'm here," Jesus said. "I've come to seek out and save the lost. Zacchaeus was lost, but now he's found!"

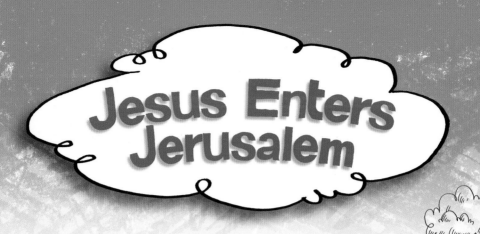

Jesus Enters Jerusalem

It was time to celebrate Passover in Jerusalem. When Jesus and the disciples arrived just outside Jerusalem, Jesus sent the disciples to get a colt.

Jesus rode the colt into Jerusalem. Huge crowds were there for the Passover festival.

"Hosanna!" the people shouted when they saw Jesus. "You are blessed!"

The people covered the road with coats and palm branches. "Jesus! King!" they cheered as they waved palm branches in the air.

Color the palm branches.

The Last Supper

The disciples prepared the Passover meal for Jesus, and he came to eat with them. Jesus knew it would be the last supper they would share.

Before they ate, Jesus washed the disciples' feet. "I have come to serve you. You should go and serve others," he told them.

They sat down at the table together and prepared to eat. Jesus looked at his disciples sadly. "One of you will betray me," he said. The disciples gasped. Who would it be?

Then Jesus took the bread, blessed it, broke it, and gave it to the disciples. "This bread is my body," Jesus said. "Whenever you eat it, remember me."

Then he poured wine, gave thanks, and gave it to the disciples. "This is my blood," Jesus said. "Whenever you drink it, remember me."

Color in the tablecloth.

After supper, Jesus went with the disciples to the garden of Gethsemane.

Count how many disciples went out with Jesus.

"I know that it is late, but stay awake while I pray," he asked his friends.

While Jesus was praying, the disciples fell asleep. "Wake up! Please stay awake!" Jesus said.

Jesus prayed two more times. Each time the disciples fell asleep. Jesus sighed, then woke up his friends. "Come, it's time to go," he told them.

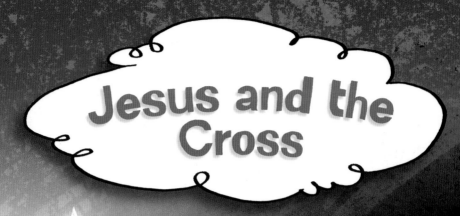

Jesus and the Cross

On that dark night, the garden of Gethsemane was quiet. The soldiers had arrested Jesus, and the disciples had run away.

The crowds were angry. They mocked and shouted at Jesus.

The soldiers had paid Judas thirty silver coins to betray Jesus.

The soldiers hurt Jesus and put a crown of thorns on his head. They forced him to carry a heavy cross.

"Crucify him!" the crowds yelled.

Jesus groaned and carried his cross up the hill.

The soldiers drove nails through Jesus' hands and feet. They hung him on the cross between two thieves.

Jesus gave a loud cry: "My God, why have you forsaken me?" And he died.

Jesus' friends took his body, wrapped him in a clean cloth, and laid him in a tomb. They said goodbye, sealing the tomb with a large stone.
It was the darkest it had ever been.

The Empty Tomb

Mary Magdalene was sadder than she had ever been. It had been three days since her friend Jesus died, and she missed him very much!

Mary and her friend went to visit Jesus' tomb. They brought spices to put on Jesus' body.

But when the two friends
arrived at the tomb
early that morning, they found . . .

NOTHING.

The stone had been rolled away! Astonished and frightened, they looked inside. Jesus' body was not there. The tomb was empty!

An angel appeared. "Do not be afraid," the angel said. "Your friend Jesus is not here. He has risen from the dead!"

The two women hurried away to share what they had seen.

"Do not be afraid," Jesus said. "Go and tell the disciples I will see them in Galilee."

Thomas Believes

The disciples were sad and afraid. Jesus had died, and they were worried they might be in trouble for being his disciples. They hid in a locked room. All of them were there, except Thomas.

291

Suddenly Jesus appeared in the room with them! The disciples jumped in surprise and joy! How could Jesus be here—alive—in a locked room?

"Peace be with you," Jesus said. He showed his disciples the wounds in his hands and side. The disciples' mouths hung open. It was really Jesus! Alive again!

Circle the wounds in Jesus' hands.

One week later, ALL the disciples hid in the locked room, including Thomas. Jesus appeared again!

"Peace be with you," Jesus said. Thomas saw the wounds in Jesus' hands and side. "Jesus, it's really you!" he exclaimed.

"You believe because you have seen," Jesus said. "Blessed are those who believe without seeing."

Breakfast with Jesus

Some of the disciples fished all night but didn't catch anything! By morning, their bellies were as empty as their nets. And it was time for breakfast!

As the sun rose, the disciples heard a voice from the shore: "You haven't caught any fish, have you?"

"Not one all night!" they called back.

"Throw your nets out again on the other side of the boat!" the voice told them.

With a gentle swoosh, they dropped their nets in the water one more time. Immediately, fish came swimming and splashing and jumping into the nets!

There were so many fish, the disciples could barely lift them! With a heave and a grunt, they pulled the fish into the boat. Not just ten fish or twenty, but 153!

Draw some fish leaping toward the boat.

As flopping fish filled the boat, the disciples realized the voice belonged to Jesus! They paddled back to shore.

Jesus sat by a small fire, toasting bread and fish for breakfast. He shared with the exhausted fishermen. The disciples munched their breakfast, filled with awe that Jesus was alive again.

The Road to
Emmaus

After Jesus died, Cleopas and his friend were walking along the road to Emmaus. They talked about how Jesus had died, and they wondered if he was really alive again.

As they walked, another man joined them. "What's wrong?" the stranger asked them.

"Have you not heard about Jesus?" they replied.

"He was crucified and died," Cleopas and his friend told the stranger. "But this morning, some of his followers say they saw Jesus alive!"

"Didn't the prophets say that God's Son would die and rise again?" the stranger asked.

305

As evening came, Cleopas and his friend invited the stranger to stay at their house. They went inside to eat. The man broke the bread, blessed it, and gave it to them.

Suddenly, they realized this stranger was Jesus! He really was alive again!

The Great Call

The disciples were filled with hope. Mary Magdalene had seen Jesus—alive! She told them Jesus wanted to meet them in Galilee, so they hurried off to see him.

Up high on a mountain peak in Galilee, Jesus appeared to the disciples. They rejoiced to see their friend and worshipped him.

Then Jesus spoke. "You have faithfully followed me, but now it's your turn. I am giving you the authority to teach and baptize in my name."

Color the woman being baptized.

"Travel near and far. Tell people about me! Baptize them in the name of the Father, Son, and Holy Spirit."

"Spread the good news of God's love. Make disciples, and teach them to obey my commandments. I will always be with you."

The disciples traveled near and far.
They shared the good news of
God's love and made disciples in
nations everywhere.

Jesus Ascends

The disciples whispered in hushed voices.
"Jesus died!" one said. "Can he really be alive again?"

"But Mary and her friend saw him," another added. "Maybe it IS true!"

"Peace be with you," Jesus said.

It SOUNDED like Jesus. The disciples peeked out from their hiding places. It LOOKED like Jesus. "Why are you afraid?" Jesus said. "I'm not a ghost. Please bring me something to eat."

315

The disciples gave Jesus a broiled fish.
With a bite and a swallow, he ate it right up.
Everyone was amazed—ghosts can't eat!
It really WAS Jesus!

Jesus told them, "Everything the prophets wrote has come true. I died, but now I am alive again! You have seen it, and you believe!"

The disciples followed Jesus as he climbed up a hill near Bethany. As Jesus blessed them, he was carried up to heaven.

The disciples worshipped Jesus and were filled with great joy. It was the last time they would see Jesus. But they were excited to share the good news of God's love with everyone!

The Holy Spirit

The disciples were gathered in a house in Jerusalem to celebrate the festival of Pentecost.

WHOOSH! A loud gust of wind blew through the house.

Flames of fire flickered above each of the disciples' heads, but the flames didn't burn them!

Color the flames of the Holy Spirit.

Filled with the Holy Spirit, the disciples began to speak in languages they had never learned before. Each spoke a different language, but they could understand one another.

Crowds of people heard the wind and gathered around the house.

All the people in the crowd understood the disciples' words in their own language!

Peter told them, "We are able to speak in many different languages because the Holy Spirit has made it possible!"

Those who heard Peter's words were baptized and welcomed as followers of Jesus—3,000 people were baptized that day!

Philip and the Ethiopian

God had a job for the disciple Philip. An angel told Philip to go to the road south of Jerusalem.

The road was in the middle of the wilderness, but when Philip got there, he saw an official from Ethiopia in a chariot. "Join him," the Holy Spirit whispered to Philip.

Color the disciple Philip.

Philip approached the man. He listened as the man read aloud from the prophet Isaiah.

"Do you understand what you're reading?" Philip asked.

"No. Can you explain it to me?" the Ethiopian said.

"I'm from Ethiopia," the man explained. "I work for the queen. I've read what the prophets wrote, but the words don't make sense to me."

Philip rode with the official in his chariot and told him the good news that, though Jesus had died, he had risen again—for us!

When they were near some water, the Ethiopian stopped the chariot and asked, "Could I be baptized now?" The two men jumped off the chariot and waded into the water.

Philip baptized the Ethiopian. Soon after, God snatched Philip away and sent him to tell others about Jesus.

The Ethiopian traveled home, rejoicing at the good news he had heard.

Saul Meets Jesus

Saul was a bully, and he did NOT like Christians. He tried to STOP anyone from sharing the story of Jesus.

When Saul met followers of Jesus, he arrested them and put them in jail.

While Saul was traveling to Damascus to arrest more Christians, he saw a bright FLASH of light and fell to the ground.

A voice said, "Saul, why do you treat me this way?" "Who are you?" Saul asked. "I am Jesus," the voice replied. "Go into the city and wait. You will be told what to do."

When Saul stood up, he couldn't see. With help, he arrived in Damascus, where he waited for Jesus. He didn't eat. He didn't drink. He only prayed.

Jesus sent his disciple Ananias to visit Saul.

Ananias placed his hands on Saul, and Saul was filled with the Holy Spirit. Scales fell from his eyes, and he could see!

Saul's heart changed, and he was baptized. He began to tell everyone the good news of Jesus. When Saul traveled and taught about Jesus, he was known as Paul.

Peter Raises Tabitha

In the town of Joppa lived a kind woman named Tabitha. She sewed clothes and gave them to the poor. She was one of Jesus' followers.

Color in the cloth Tabitha is making.

When Tabitha got sick, her friends hoped she would get better. But she died.

The disciples in Joppa sent word to Peter: "Our beloved Tabitha has died! Please come!"

Tabitha's friends missed her very much. Big, wet tears of sadness rolled down their cheeks.

They washed and covered Tabitha's body so she could be buried.

Peter arrived in Joppa and went to Tabitha's room. He asked everyone to go outside. After they left, Peter prayed.

"Tabitha, stand up!" Peter commanded. Tabitha opened her eyes and smiled. Peter helped her to her feet. Tabitha was alive again! God had answered Peter's prayer.

Together, Peter and Tabitha walked outside. Tabitha's friends cheered and cried tears of happiness. The story spread throughout Joppa, and many who heard it believed.

Paul and Silas

Paul and his friend Silas traveled
many places to tell people about
Jesus. They were happy to spread
the good news. But not everyone
took joy in hearing it.

In a marketplace, Paul and Silas angered
some of the leaders of Rome,
who saw Jesus as a troublemaker.

The Roman guards hauled Paul and Silas off to jail. But they remained faithful. They prayed and sang hymns to God. The other prisoners listened.

That night, an earthquake shook all the jail doors open. The jailer woke up and ran to look for the prisoners. If they escaped, he would be in big trouble.

But Paul and Silas and all the other prisoners had stayed in their cells. The jailer fell to his knees in front of Paul and Silas. "What must I do to be saved?" he asked them.

"Believe in Jesus," Paul and Silas told him. The jailer and all of his family were baptized.

List of Stories and Scripture References

The Parable of the House on the Rock	Matthew 7:24-27
The Parable of the Sower	Matthew 13:3-9, 18-23
The Parable of the Mustard Seed	Mark 4:30-32
The Parable of the Good Samaritan	Luke 10:25-37
The Parable of the Prodigal Son	Luke 15:11-32
Jesus Walks on Water	Matthew 14:22-33
A Man through the Roof	Luke 5:17-26
The Ten Outcasts	Luke 17:11-19
Jesus Feeds 5,000	John 6:1-14
Lazarus	John 11:1-45
The Lord's Prayer	Matthew 6:5-15
Jesus and the Children	Mark 10:13-16
The Widow's Offering	Mark 12:41-44
Mary and Martha	Luke 10:38-42
Zacchaeus the Tax Collector	Luke 19:1-10
Jesus Enters Jerusalem	Luke 19:28-40
The Last Supper	Matthew 26:26-30, 36-46
Jesus and the Cross	Matthew 27: 27-61
The Empty Tomb	Luke 24:1-12
Thomas Believes	John 20:19-29
Breakfast with Jesus	John 21:1-14